I love reading

My Cat Has Had Kittens

by Leonie Bennett

Editorial consultant: Mitch Cronick

ticktock

Copyright © **ticktock Entertainment Ltd 2006**
First published in Great Britain in 2006 by **ticktock Media Ltd.,**
Unit 2, Orchard Business Centre, North Farm Road, Tunbridge Wells, Kent TN2 3XF

We would like to thank: Shirley Bickler and Suzanne Baker

ISBN 1 86007 977 6 pbk
Printed in China

Picture credits
t=top, b=bottom, c=center, l-left, r=right, OFC= outside front cover
Marilyn Storey at Skidoosh British Shorthaired Cats: OFC, 1, 2, 5, 6, 8t, 9, 10-11, 12, 13, 14, 15, 16, 17, 18, 19, 21. Superstock: 4, 8b, 20.

CONTENTS

My cat Sophie

Sophie is a silver tabby cat.

She is two years old.

Sophie has a fat tummy.

Going to the vet

The vet checks that
Sophie is not ill.

He looks in Sophie's
eyes and ears.

He feels Sophie's tummy.

Sophie is going to
have kittens.

Vet

Sophie's special place

Sophie looks for somewhere to have her kittens.

The garden is too cold.

The kitchen is too noisy.

This big box is just right.

It is warm. It is quiet.

Wow – my cat's a mom!

Here are the new kittens.

There are four kittens.

The kittens drink milk from Sophie.

Then they go to sleep.

Look at the new kittens

The kittens are three days old.

They can't see.
They can't walk.

The kittens sleep a lot.

They sleep together to keep warm.

Watching the kittens grow

Now the kittens are two weeks old.

They can see.

They can walk.

Soon they use the litter box.

Sophie licks the kittens to keep them clean.

Growing up

Now the kittens are four weeks old.

They can eat solid food.

This kitten is
the biggest.

He eats a lot.

The kittens like to play with
Sophie's tail.

Busy kittens

Now the kittens are ten weeks old.

They run about.

They play and fight.

They like to bite.

They like to lick.

Look out! Kittens like to scratch.

Saying goodbye

Two of the kittens are going to new homes.

I say goodbye to them.

Now Sophie has just two kittens.

Soon they will go to live in new homes.

But I will keep Sophie.

Yes or no?
Talking about kittens

Sophie has six kittens.

Yes or no?

Kittens like to play.

Yes or no?

Kittens can see when they are born.

Yes or no?

Kittens can't
walk when
they are born.

Yes or no?

What game would you
play with a kitten?

Activities

What did you think of this book?

 Brilliant **Good** **OK**

Which page did you like best? Why?

· · · · · · · · · · · · · · ·

Put these words in the right order:

going • kittens. • Sophie • is • have • to

· · · · · · · · · · · · · · ·

Make a "Welcome Home" card for a new kitten.

· · · · · · · · · · · · · · ·

Who is the author of this book?
Have you read *My Dog Has Had Puppies* by the same author?